Carla Vetere

CICERO

FROM THE PAST

TO THE FUTURE

Culture and politics

in Cicero's *De Oratore*

Index

PREFACE

This text, elaborated with competence and mastery by prof. Carla Vetere, should be read and commented on in all high schools. It is an epitome of life and thought of a scholar who tried to bring the best of Greek culture to Rome.

Through a deep reflection on Hellenic culture, of which he proposed an original redrafting while respecting the system of values of his country, Cicero outlined the figure of the ideal Statesman, the *Orator*, who joins together legal science, wide general knowledge and practical experience.

This should be the mission of the School: to train young people to spend their lives in the name of high ideals and to proudly carry the heritage of experience and discipline, learned in years of life together, which are the result of a combination of Greco-Roman culture handed down to us from our traditions starting from Cicero's writings, ideas and thoughts.

The challenge is more relevant than ever; the whole School should be able to proudly affirm "I prepare for life and arms" - which is the motto of the Military School 'Nunziatella' of Naples, the 'Rosso Maniero' proud of its more than bicentenary tradition and vocation to the training of young people – because the common goal should be the formation of good citizens and the most powerful weapons ever are those of the culture and of the high values.

Francesco Sciascia

Retired Colonel, National Vice President of the Alumni Association of the "Nunziatella" Military School of Naples, student of the 1954/57 course, and officer at the "Nunziatella" from 1974 to 1988.

INTRODUCTION

Cicero and us

Why reading Cicero today? This is the most frequently asked question by my students in high school or by my interlocutors during conferences or literary conversations. I think that's the question all those who don't read this author ask themselves. The real problem is that there is not a single answer because the reason becomes evident *ex post*, after reading a work by Cicero and not before, and it depends on the experience and expectations of the reader with respect to this giant of the literature.

The *De Oratore* in particular is a work rich in themes and extremely articulate, so I can say why I choose, among countless ancient works, this for talking about the relationship between culture and politics. The reason is that by accident I found it in my hands during the Covid-19 emergency, at a time when world politics has faced many problems at a same time and the sum has been emotionally, economically, psychologically, socially devastating. I was wondering why politicians gave answers so far from each other on the same topics and why some of these answers were so often so far from common opinions. I asked myself what I expect from a politician, how I wish he/she reasoned, what kind of image I wanted my country gave to the rest of the world. These are basically fairly elementary questions which however concern political philosophy. Well, Cicero gave a possible answer to these questions of mine and called into question the skilled political philosophers to call them back to the need to abandon abstract questions and to deal actively and proactively with the real facts, all those who, as Machiavelli stated in chapter XV of "The Prince", constitute the "actual truth". Needless to pretend to live in a non-existent world, and to think about abstract things, we have to deal with the problems we face from time to time and analyse them correctly to direct our action.

This is why Cicero has a lot to do with me and with all of us: because he has long thought on similar problems - it is clear: not the same - as ours;

these are issues that are part of our being 'human' and Cicero has tried to give answers, to identify a method and practical tools to read reality, honestly declaring that he does not possess the truth but that he is willing to follow the path that leads to it. Just as clearly, by choosing the form of a dialogue, he expressed his intention not to proceed alone, but to walk with others. This is why he compares different ideas through different characters. In these men, perhaps, each of us will find some element of his/her own way of thinking and feeling.

Carla Vetere

From the past to the future:

culture and politics in Cicero's *De Oratore*

The theme of this short essay is the relationship between culture and politics and how this relationship was configured in a historical period, the first century BC, in which the Roman *Res Publica* was undergoing epochal transformations that would have brought to the principality of Augustus and, therefore, to a new State configuration: the empire. I believe that some considerations on that historical moment can make us reflect on our time and on the ongoing changes, for this reason I will try to make some notes that refer directly to the present. Talking about the present also means talking about the future, because it is in the present that we build what will be and we determine, within the limits in which it is allowed to us, our destiny.

In order to examine the proposed theme, I decided to resort to Cicero with specific reasons.

1) Cicero was not only a witness, but a protagonist of the political events of his time. He lived at the time of Gaius Marius, of whom he was countryman and was a little younger, and attended all of Sulla's political parable. Many conflicts took place during his life: the Jugurthine war, the violent rivalry between Marius and Sulla, the social war, the civil war. He was perhaps the greatest orator of antiquity, but also a politician, who started as *homo novus* from a small town, like Arpino, who accomplished all the *cursus honorum* and arrived at the highest office: the consulate. As a consul he had the need to face the real possibility of a coup. Everyone remembers the conspiracy of Catiline; but he also had to confront a political giant named Caesar, the one who changed the history and the destinies of Rome.

2) Cicero on several occasions dealt with the relationship between culture and politics. Among his many works, the one of which the great political importance is recognized, is, despite the title, the *De Oratore*. To use Augusto Rostagni's words: «*De Oratore* is a political work because it deals with the concrete organization of the State and with the

importance of the role of eloquence in social life»
(Introduction to *De Oratore*, ed. UTET)

The *De Oratore* was composed between 57 and 55 BC and is a dialogue set on the occasion of the *Roman Ludi* (between 4 and 12 September) of 91 BC in the villa of Tusculum by the great orator Lucius Licinius Crassus. Crassus's interlocutors are Marcus Antonius (orator), grandfather of the famous triumvir, Quintus Mucius Scaevola Augur and, to a lesser extent, Lutatius Catulus and Julius Caesar Strabo.

The interlocutors have in common the fact of being aristocrats of blood and by intimate conviction; in addition, they are men faithful to the Roman tradition and enemies of tumultuous and disordered life.

The Orator whom Cicero outlines through the dialogue is not only a lawyer because he is not only concerned with defending private individuals in their daily procedural activities. Through the words of Lucius Licinius Crassus it is understood that the Orator is first and foremost a politician. In I, 214 Antonius explicitly says that «Crassus handed over the helm of the State to the Orator» («Crassus ... civitatum regendarum oratori gubernacula sententia sua tradidit»). Moreover Crassus himself says (I, 30 ff) that «Nothing is more prestigious of the ability to captivate people with speech, gain the consensus, push them at will wherever and by anywhere at will deter them», and adds that (I, 32 -33) «The speech of one man can change the passions of the people, the scruples of the judges, the inflexibility of the Senate».

It is clear that here we find the 3 great actors of politics at the time of Cicero: the people, the judges and the central government. It seems to me that these are even now the «architects of politics».

The Orator then has the ability to «<u>give relief to supplicants, raise the afflicted, save lives, free from dangers, remove the citizens from exile</u>» (I,32: «quid tam porro regium tam liberale tam munificum quam opem ferre supplicibus, excitare adflictos, dare salutem, liberare periculis, retinere omnes in civitate?»). Cicero uses analogous words in *Pro Archia* §13: «ex iis studiis quoque crescit oratio et facultas quae…numquam amicorum periculis defuit»; §16: «haec studia…adversis perfugium ac solacium praebent».

I would say that these are all elements of concrete political action, because it is the task of politics, especially in these days of emergency, it is precisely that of giving answers to citizens in difficulty, which in our time are linked above all to several great themes: economics, safety and legal certainty.

Cicero strengthens the concept and says (I, 34) «In the wise guidance of an accomplished Orator lies the foundation not only of his personal prestige, but also of the salvation of many citizens and of the whole State» («perfecti oratoris moderatione et sapientia non solum ipsius dignitatem sed et privatorum plurimorum et universae rei publicae salutem maxime contineri»). Therefore, he urges young people to dedicate themselves to the oratory so as to bring glory to themselves, to be useful to friends and to bring concrete benefits to the State («ut et vobis honori et amicis utilitati et rei publicae emolumento esse possitis»).

This statement is relevant also for the politician, who should have such preparation and authority to determine not only his individual success, earned by attending the forum - today we would say: going on TV - but also to guide the State efficiently and effectively as a whole and to meet the contingent needs of citizens when they find themselves in difficulty.

Crassus is convinced that a great culture is needed to create such a figure. And here arises a heated dispute but always very polite between Crassus and Antonius in which Scaevola also fits.

For Crassus, the Orator must have knowledge in practically all fields of knowledge, because these can come in handy in his daily activity. To those who reproach him that only a technician can speak about a certain subject, Crassus replies that the Orator is like a poet who often deals with topics he does not know but, once learned, he is able to expose them in a clear, complete and adorned way: this will never be possible for a technician, no matter how good. For example, Nicander of Colophon wrote three technical works, known to Virgil himself, about ferocious beasts, about remedies for poisons, and about the life of the fields («Gheorghicà») (I, 70: «est enim finitimus oratori poeta, numeris adstrictior paulo, verborum autem licentia liberior, multis vero ornandi generibus socius ac paene par; in hoc quidem certe proprie idem, nullis ut terminis circumscribat aut definiat ius suum, quo minus ei liceat eadem illa facultate et copia vagari qua velit » - « the poet is a close relative of the Orator: a little more conditioned by the metre, but freer and bolder in his lexical choice, he is a companion and almost a relative for the wealth of ornaments; in one aspect he identifies with him: in not placing to his own ability limits or boundaries that preclude him from moving freely anywhere, at will with the same ingenuity and the same expressive richness»)

Now it is well understood that this culture was certainly not necessary for a normal forensic activity, but it could be very useful to the politician who had to be able to make decisions and, therefore, to create a personal judgment, on extremely varied subjects.

Crassus adds one more remark regarding the liberal arts (I, 73): «even if we do not use them when speaking, they nevertheless appear and is evident if we are unaware or if we have learned them» («iis artibus, qae sunt libero dignae ... ipsis si in dicendo non utimur, tamen apparet atque extat, utrum simus earum rudes an didicerimus»).

In essence, culture naturally confers authority on those who own it because our way of being, our behaviour shows what we have made our own, what has entered our human baggage, without the need to show off. <u>Culture is an attitude (*habitus*)</u>

Also this concept will be briefly taken up again to be further strengthened in the *Pro Archia*, wherein Cicero states that it is true that nature often proves more important than doctrine to obtain glory and honor (which correspond to the great aspirations of the ancient Greeks: kléos and timé) but an extraordinarily gifted nature is exalted and brought to perfection by culture (§15: «cum ad naturam eximiam et illustrem accesserit ratio quaedam conformatioque doctrinae, tum illud nescio quid praeclarum ac singulare solere existere»)

The Orator then, as a politician and man of culture to whom everyone looks, must be skilled as an actor, must take care of the gesture 'actio' and the way he speaks because «quotiens enim dicimus, totiens de nobis iudicatur» (I, 125) «Every time we speak, as many times others form a judgment about us».

And here too I would like to point out that prudence and the ability to express oneself, in essence the ability to communicate correctly, are fundamental gifts for those who must manage public affairs.

Antonius is in fact convinced that the Orator needs more natural skills than the culture, which cannot be learnt from manuals. What we would call 'soft skills', that is social skills, as well as the ability to convince others in part are naturally possessed, in part are learnt with concrete experience, being among the people and learning to intercept their moods and then exploit them to your advantage in building a speech that affects the audience in its weak points. The Orator must convince the judges in every way, pretend to inform them correctly (*docere*), but in reality bend them to his own will (*conciliare et movere*).

Antonius' speech lends itself to a double reading.

1) The first foresees a political use of right and of laws, using and trying to enforce the rules that are most convenient in the particular circumstance.

2) The second, necessary reading is this: let us never forget the precept «summum ius, summa iniuria». A knowledge and an appropriate use of the rules allows to avoid injustices. At the basis of everything, and above all the application of the rules, there must be Justice with a capital letter and common sense. A statement still true today and revolutionary.

Scaevola reiterates Antonius' speech and highlights the dangers of eloquence and of a badly addressed culture; in fact he says that States were founded by wise and energetic men. He recalls the case of Romulus, endowed with *consilium et sapientia*, but not eloquence (I, 37) and the even more striking case of the censor Tiberius Sempronius Gracchus (220-154 BC) father of the most famous tribunes. He was *prudens et gravis, haudquaquam eloquens* (I, 38) who contributed significantly to the restoration of the internal order by distributing the freedmen in the various tribes, and also to the affirmation of the Romans on the international scene.

On the contrary, Scaevola recalls, his sons Tiberius and Gaius were men of supreme eloquence (I, 38 *eloquentissimos*) and equipped with every resource both natural and acquired through the study (I, 39 «diserti et omnibus vel naturae vel doctrinae praesidiis ad dicendum parati»), and they received an extremely flourishing State thanks to the paternal prudence and to the armies of their ancestors («vel paterno consilio vel avitis armis»), but thanks to their utmost eloquence they destroyed public affairs. And here Cicero uses an expression that indicates the squandering of a patrimony («eloquentia rem publicam dissipaverunt»), and he does it consciously because the Orator was convinced that a healthy State was a common patrimony difficult to obtain, but too much easy to dispel.

In other words, the danger of putting culture and eloquence in the wrong hands is taking shape here. Culture is like a tool that can be used to build as well as to destroy, to defend himself as to offend. The Gracchi brothers had the limit, from Cicero's point of view, of course, to have little foresight and prudence, political myopia and ideals of justice so abstract as to make them impractical and dangerous. In their hands, eloquence had been a means of destruction.

Crassus will resume Scaevola's speech to affirm with the utmost decision in the third book of *De Oratore* that if wisdom and honesty are lacking, the oratory art becomes a very serious danger. Oratory, understood as a set of vast knowledge and ability to render it with eloquent words, <u>is not a morally neutral instrument</u>.

I would say that it is still today. We speak of demagogy when we want to emphasize a discourse that does not have at its centre the common good but particular interests or wrong means or purposes. Cicero speaks of incorrect use of the tools provided by culture and nature (*natura et doctrina*).

This problem for Cicero was particularly felt because it had influenced his life and that of his brother Quintus to whom *De Oratore* is dedicated. The two brothers had initially been opposed at the beginning of their political career in Rome because although they were *cives*, they were also *homines novi*, that is, they had no ancestors who held public offices, therefore, from the point of view of the aristocrats they were not, so to speak, «educated to exercise power». Cicero, however, proved to be different from many other newcomers. What made the difference was his incredibly vast and varied culture and his sense of the State.

Cicero is in fact on the same line as Crassus in defending a vast and non-specialized basic training because (I, 56) «in the speech those commonplaces will arise for which we must speak of the immortal gods, the sense of duty, concord, friendship, civil law, natural law, international law, equanimity, temperance, magnanimity, all kinds of virtues» («cum illi in dicendo inciderint loci, quod persaepe evenit, ut de diis immortalibus, de pietate, de concordia, de amicitia, de communi civium, de hominum, de gentium iure, de aequitate, de temperantia, de magnitudine animi, de omni virtutis genere dicendum sit»). Basically, when you study, you practice on concrete and recurring themes. The *loci communes* are not a set of pure banalities but are recurring themes in concrete experience, in everyday life and in common history. Let's take friendship. Friendship can be declined in many ways and it is always something that is part of our being men. It is a theme that crosses the ages and peoples. The texts of the great authors are points of reference to be known and constantly confronted with, says Cicero, also to criticize and refute them. (I, 158: «We must read the poets, know the history, choose the teachers and writers of all the liberal disciplines ... correct them, criticize them, refute them» «legendi etiam poetae, cognoscendae historiae, omnium bonarum artium doctores atque scriptores et legendi et pervolutandi et exercitationis causa laudandi, interpretandi, corrigendi, vituperandi, refellendi»).

In this regard, Cicero gets angry with the philosophical schools and with some great philosophers of antiquity, guilty of abstracting too much from reality. Plato, for example, had hypothesized a form of ideal State which was not possible in reality. Cicero goes so far as to say: «Plato ... the ideas and principles that he believed he should expound on justice were far from the reality of everyday life and the customs of civil communities» (I, 224). So it is better to keep the books of philosophers for holidays and leisure.

Actually Cicero was not angry with philosophers in general. Indeed, he recalls that men like Pericles and Alexander the Great had been disciples of great philosophers like of Anaxagoras and Aristotle. Our Orator fearlessly attacks the tendency of certain philosophers to deal with the «quaestiones infinitae», that is, questions that abstractly concern the general principles, but without dealing with reality, with concrete facts and not always with honest aims.

We would say that rather than with Cicero's philosophy, it had as its target the ideology which, although apparently fascinating, leads us astray and to make mistakes when we have to make important decisions. There what matters is a culture, a preparation and an oratory capacity supported by honesty, probity, attention to reality, foresight and sense of State.

Culture, Cicero tells us, is attractive but also dangerous because often the audience is made up of uneducated and unprepared people.

The politician must be cultured and have vast and varied knowledge to better serve the State, he must be able to convince the audience with the charm of his speech which is not the useless noise that hides the absence of content, but the worthy garment of high concepts. On the other hand, without knowledge of men and of situations and without high moral values, without *consilium, sapientia, gravitas et prudentia*, the politician will never be able to hold straight the helm of the State.

Notes

The edition of the text from which the quotations of *De Oratore* are taken is by Emanuele Narducci, *Dell'Oratore*, BUR 1997

The edition of the text from which the quotations of

the oration *Pro Archia* are taken is by Emanuele

Narducci, *Il poeta Archia*, BUR 2018

MINIMAL ANTHOLOGY

To allow the reading and meditation of the texts mentioned in the essay and to facilitate their correct contextualization, the most relevant chapters of the first and third books of *De Oratore* are proposed, preceded by short introductory sections.

The texts are taken from the following sites:

http://www.thelatinlibrary.com/cicero/oratore1.shtml;

http://www.thelatinlibrary.com/cicero/oratore3.shtml

In the following chapters - taken from Book I, XI-XIII - the orator Marcus Licinius Crassus clearly explains the reasons why he is convinced that the orator must have a vast and profound culture. The general criterion is «dicendi enim virtus, nisi ei qui dicet et ea quae dicet percepta sunt, extare non potest» («the full ability to speak, cannot be sustained if arguments of which is about to speak are not well-known to the person who will speak»).

On the other hand, perfect knowledge of the topics to be treated is also common to philosophers - and Crassus cites personalities of the caliber of Aristotle, Theophrastus and Carneades - but in order to deal arguments in a pleasant and elegant way, philosophers also needed to master the *ars dicendi*. So to avoid the «verborum sonitus inanis» («the empty sound of words alone») two elements are necessary: the mastery of the topic and the ability to express themselves appropriately and elegantly. In fact, «nulla subiecta sententia nec scientia» («if there is no solid knowledge of the subject») the speech will be empty and even worthy of derision; if, on the other hand, there is no way of expressing itself that can intercept and attract the sensitivity of the audience («oratio gravis et ornata et hominum sensibus ac mentibus accommodata»), the public will not pay attention and even the best argument is likely to technically remain empty words.

[XI] [45] Tum ille "non sum" inquit "nescius, Scaevola, ista inter Graecos dici et disceptari solere; audivi enim summos homines, cum quaestor ex Macedonia venissem Athenas, florente Academia, ut temporibus illis ferebatur, cum eam Charmadas et Clitomachus et Aeschines obtinebant; erat etiam Metrodorus, qui cum illis una ipsum illum Carneadem diligentius audierat, hominem omnium in dicendo, ut ferebant, acerrimum et copiosissimum; vigebatque auditor Panaeti illius tui Mnesarchus et Peripatetici Critolai Diodorus; [46] multi erant praeterea clari in philosophia et nobiles, a quibus omnibus una paene voce repelli oratorem a gubernaculis civitatum, excludi ab omni doctrina rerumque maiorum scientia ac tantum in iudicia et contiunculas tamquam in aliquod pistrinum detrudi et compingi videbam; [47] sed ego neque illis adsentiebar neque harum disputationum inventori et principi longe omnium in dicendo gravissimo et eloquentissimo, Platoni, cuius tum Athenis cum Charmada diligentius legi Gorgiam; quo in libro in hoc maxime admirabar Platonem, quod mihi [in] oratoribus inridendis ipse esse orator summus videbatur. Verbi enim controversia iam diu torquet

Graeculos homines contentionis cupidiores quam veritatis. [48] Nam si quis hunc statuit esse oratorem, qui tantummodo in iure aut in iudiciis possit aut apud populum aut in senatu copiose loqui, tamen huic ipsi multa tribuat et concedat necesse est; neque enim sine multa pertractatione omnium rerum publicarum neque sine legum, morum, iuris scientia neque natura hominum incognita ac moribus in his ipsis rebus satis callide versari et perite potest; qui autem haec cognoverit, sine quibus ne illa quidem minima in causis quisquam recte tueri potest, quid huic abesse poterit de maximarum rerum scientia? Sin oratoris nihil vis esse nisi composite, ornate, copiose loqui, quaero, id ipsum qui possit adsequi sine ea scientia, quam ei non conceditis? Dicendi enim virtus, nisi ei, qui dicet, ea, quae dicet, percepta sunt, exstare non potest. [49] Quam ob rem, si ornate locutus est, sicut et fertur et mihi videtur, physicus ille Democritus, materies illa fuit physici,, de qua dixit, ornatus vero ipse verborum oratoris putandus est; et, si Plato de rebus ab civilibus controversiis remotissimis divinitus est locutus, quod ego concedo; si item Aristoteles, si Theophrastus, si Carneades in rebus eis, de quibus disputaverunt, eloquentes et in dicendo suaves atque ornati fuerunt, sint eae res, de quibus disputant, in aliis quibusdam studiis, oratio quidem ipsa propria est huius unius rationis, de qua loquimur et quaerimus. [50] Etenim videmus eisdem de rebus ieiune quosdam et exiliter, ut eum, quem acutissimum ferunt, Chrysippum, disputavisse neque ob eam rem philosophiae non satis fecisse, quod non habuerit hanc dicendi ex arte aliena facultatem.

[XII] Quid ergo interest aut qui discernes eorum, quos nominavi, in dicendo ubertatem et copiam ab eorum exilitate, qui hac dicendi varietate et elegantia non utuntur? Vnum erit profecto, quod ei, qui bene dicunt, adferunt proprium, compositam orationem et ornatam et artificio quodam et expolitione distinctam; haec autem oratio, si res non subest ab oratore percepta et cognita, aut nulla sit necesse est aut omnium inrisione ludatur. [51] Quid est enim tam furiosum, quam verborum vel optimorum atque ornatissimorum sonitus inanis, nulla subiecta sententia nec scientia? Quicquid erit igitur quacumque ex arte, quocumque de genere, orator id, si tamquam clientis causam didicerit, dicet melius et ornatius quam ipse ille eius rei inventor atque artifex. [52] Nam si quis erit qui hoc dicat, esse quasdam oratorum proprias sententias atque causas et certarum rerum forensibus cancellis circumscriptam scientiam, fatebor equidem in his magis adsidue versari hanc nostram dictionem, sed tamen in his ipsis rebus permulta sunt, quae ipsi magistri, qui rhetorici vocantur, nec tradunt nec tenent. [53] Quis enim nescit maximam vim exsistere oratoris in hominum mentibus vel ad iram aut ad odium aut ad dolorem incitandis vel ab hisce eisdem permotionibus ad lenitatem misericordiamque revocandis? Quae nisi qui naturas hominum vimque omnem humanitatis causasque eas, quibus mentes aut incitantur aut reflectuntur, penitus perspexerit, dicendo quod volet perficere non poterit. [54] Atque totus hic locus philosophorum proprius videtur, neque orator me auctore umquam repugnabit; sed, cum illis cognitionem rerum concesserit, quod in ea solum illi voluerint elaborare, tractationem orationis, quae sine illa scientia est nulla, sibi adsumet; hoc enim est proprium oratoris, quod saepe iam dixi, oratio gravis et ornata et hominum sensibus ac mentibus accommodata.

[XIII] [55] Quibus de rebus Aristotelem et Theophrastum scripsisse fateor; sed vide ne hoc, Scaevola, totum sit a me: nam ego, quae sunt oratori cum illis communia, non mutuor ab illis, isti quae de his rebus disputant, oratorum esse concedunt, itaque ceteros libros artis suae nomine, hos rhetoricos et inscribunt et appellant. [56] Etenim cum illi in dicendo inciderint loci, quod persaepe evenit, ut de dis immortalibus, de pietate, de concordia, de amicitia, de communi civium, de hominum, de gentium iure, de aequitate, de temperantia, de magnitudine animi, de omni virtutis genere sit dicendum, clamabunt, credo, omnia gymnasia atque omnes philosophorum scholae sua esse haec omnia propria, nihil omnino ad oratorem pertinere; [57] quibus ego, ut de his rebus in angulis consumendi oti causa disserant, cum concessero, illud tamen oratori tribuam et dabo, ut eadem, de quibus illi tenui quodam exsanguique sermone disputant, hic cum omni iucunditate et gravitate explicet. Haec ego cum ipsis philosophis [tum] Athenis disserebam; cogebat enim me M. Marcellus hic noster, qui [nunc aedilis curulis est et] profecto, nisi ludos nunc faceret, huic nostro sermoni interesset; ac iam tum erat adulescentulus his studiis mirifice deditus. [58] Iam vero de legibus constituendis, de bello, de pace, de sociis, de vectigalibus, de iure civium generatim in ordines aetatesque discriptorum dicant vel Graeci, si volunt, Lycurgum aut Solonem - quamquam illos quidem censemus in numero eloquentium reponendos - scisse melius quam Hyperidem aut Demosthenem, perfectos iam homines in dicendo et perpolitos, vel nostri decem viros, qui XII tabulas perscripserunt, quos necesse est fuisse prudentis, anteponant in hoc genere et Ser. Galbae et socero tuo C. Laelio, quos constat dicendi gloria praestitisse. [59] Numquam enim negabo esse quasdam partis proprias eorum, qui in his cognoscendis atque tractandis studium suum omne posuerunt, sed oratorem plenum atque perfectum esse eum, qui de omnibus rebus possit copiose varieque dicere.

In chapters XIV and XV of the First book, Marcus Licinius Crassus proposes to answer an obvious and quite frequent objection: whether or not it is possible to speak adequately about a topic without knowing it well.

In line with the rest of his arguments Crassus replies that it is impossible, but wisely adds also that the basic culture of an orator cannot embrace all knowledge, thus he must have acquired the ability to gain knowledge all topics to be treated by specialists, so as to be able to exhibit the matter better than specialists themselves!

This observation is truly significant, because it indicates that the orator has above all a consolidated method of learning, which allows him to approach any knowledge and to become able to master it: this is an observation valid at all times, a gold currency that the classic Cicero transmits to posterity.

XIV] Etenim saepe in eis causis, quas omnes proprias esse oratorum confitentur, est aliquid, quod non ex usu forensi, quem solum oratoribus conceditis, sed ex obscuriore aliqua scientia sit promendum atque sumendum. [60] Quaero enim num possit aut contra imperatorem aut pro imperatore dici sine rei militaris usu aut saepe etiam sine regionum terrestrium aut maritimarum scientia; num apud populum de legibus iubendis aut vetandis, num in senatu de omni rei publicae genere dici sine summa rerum civilium cognitione et prudentia; num admoveri possit oratio ad sensus animorum atque motus vel inflammandos vel etiam exstinguendos, quod unum in oratore dominatur, sine diligentissima pervestigatione earum omnium rationum, quae de naturis humani generis ac moribus a philosophis explicantur.[61] Atque haud scio an minus vobis hoc sim probaturus; equidem non dubitabo, quod sentio, dicere: physica ista ipsa et mathematica et quae paulo ante ceterarum artium propria posuisti, scientiae sunt eorum, qui illa profitentur, inlustrari autem oratione si quis istas ipsas artis velit, ad oratoris ei confugiendum est facultatem. [62] Neque enim si Philonem illum architectum, qui Atheniensibus armamentarium fecit, constat perdiserte populo rationem operis sui reddidisse, existimandum est architecti potius artificio disertum quam oratoris fuisse; nec, si huic M. Antonio pro Hermodoro fuisset de navalium opere dicendum, non, cum ab illo causam didicisset, ipse ornate de alieno artificio copioseque dixisset; neque vero Asclepiades, is quo nos medico amicoque usi sumus tum eloquentia vincebat ceteros medicos, in eo ipso, quod ornate dicebat, medicinae facultate utebatur, non eloquentiae. [63] Atque illud est probabilius, neque tamen verum, quod Socrates dicere solebat, omnis in eo, quod scirent, satis esse eloquentis; illud verius, neque quemquam in eo disertum esse posse, quod nesciat, neque, si optime sciat ignarusque sit faciundae ac poliendae orationis, diserte id ipsum, de quo sciat, posse dicere.

[XV] [64] Quam ob rem, si quis universam et propriam oratoris vim definire complectique vult, is orator erit mea sententia hoc tam gravi dignus nomine, qui, quaecumque res inciderit, quae sit dictione explicanda, prudenter et composite et ornate et memoriter dicet cum quadam actionis etiam dignitate. [65] Sin cuipiam nimis infinitum videtur, quod ita posui "quaecumque de re," licet hinc quantum cuique videbitur circumcidat atque amputet, tamen illud tenebo, si, quae ceteris in artibus atque studiis sita sunt, orator ignoret tantumque ea teneat, quae sint in disceptationibus atque usu forensi, tamen his de rebus ipsis si sit ei dicendum, cum cognoverit ab eis, qui tenent, quae sint in quaque re, multo oratorem melius quam ipsos illos, quorum eae sint artes, esse dicturum. [66] Ita si de re militari dicendum huic erit Sulpicio, quaeret a C. Mario adfini nostro et, cum acceperit, ita pronuntiabit, ut ipsi C. Mario paene hic melius quam ipse illa scire videatur; sin de iure civili, tecum communicabit, te hominem prudentissimum et peritissimum in eis ipsis rebus, quas abs te didicerit, dicendi arte superabit. [67] Sin quae res inciderit, in qua de natura, de vitiis hominum, de cupiditatibus, de modo, de continentia, de dolore, de morte dicendum sit, forsitan, si ei sit visum, - etsi haec quidem nosse debet orator -, cum Sex. Pompeio, erudito homine in philosophia, communicarit; hoc profecto efficiet ut, quamcumque rem a quoquo cognoverit, de ea multo dicat ornatius quam ille ipse, unde cognorit. [68] Sed si me audiet, quoniam philosophia in tris partis est tributa, in naturae obscuritatem, in disserendi subtilitatem, in vitam atque mores, duo illa relinquamus atque largiamur inertiae nostrae; tertium vero, quod semper oratoris fuit, nisi tenebimus, nihil oratori, in quo magnus esse possit, relinquemus. [69] Qua re hic locus de vita et moribus totus est oratori perdiscendus; cetera si non didicerit, tamen poterit, si quando opus erit, ornare dicendo, si modo ad eum erunt delata et ei tradita.

So far the orator has been compared with philosophers. The famous comparison between an orator and a poet appears in chapter XVI of the first book of *De Oratore*. Cicero, in fact, considers the orator and the poet very similar because both do not set limits on the fields of knowledge with which they can deal («in hoc quidem certe prope idem, nullis ut terminis circumscribat aut definiat ius suum, quo minus ei liceat eadem illa facultate et copia vagari qua velit»). Nicander of Colophon was a poet, certainly not a farmer, yet he wrote a splendid work on agriculture («Gheorghicà»).

These are also the paragraphs in which it is emphasized that culture, knowledge of the liberal arts, can be seen even if it is not flaunted: Cicero compares the orator to a gymnast who has graceful movements even when he is not in the gym.

[XVI] Etenim si constat inter doctos, hominem ignarum astrologiae ornatissimis atque optimis versibus Aratum de caelo stellisque dixisse; si de rebus rusticis hominem ab agro remotissimum Nicandrum Colophonium poetica quadam facultate, non rustica, scripsisse praeclare, quid est cur non orator de rebus eis eloquentissime dicat, quas ad certam causam tempusque cognorit? [70] Est enim finitimus oratori poeta, numeris astrictior paulo, verborum autem licentia liberior, multis vero ornandi generibus socius ac paene par; in hoc quidem certe prope idem, nullis ut terminis circumscribat aut definiat ius suum, quo minus ei liceat eadem illa facultate et copia vagari qua velit.[71] Nam quod illud, Scaevola, negasti te fuisse laturum, nisi in meo regno esses, quod in omni genere sermonis, in omni parte humanitatis dixerim oratorem perfectum

esse debere: numquam me hercule hoc dicerem, si eum, quem fingo, me ipsum esse arbitrarer. [72] Sed, ut solebat C. Lucilius saepe dicere, homo tibi subiratus, mihi propter eam ipsam causam minus quam volebat familiaris, sed tamen et doctus et perurbanus, sic sentio neminem esse in oratorum numero habendum, qui non sit omnibus eis artibus, quae sunt libero dignae, perpolitus; quibus ipsis si in dicendo non utimur, tamen apparet atque exstat, utrum simus earum rudes an didicerimus: [73] ut qui pila ludunt, non utuntur in ipsa lusione artificio proprio palaestrae, sed indicat ipse motus, didicerintne palaestram an nesciant, et qui aliquid fingunt, etsi tum pictura nihil utuntur, tamen, utrum sciant pingere an nesciant, non obscurum est; sic in orationibus hisce ipsis iudiciorum, contionum, senatus, etiam si proprie ceterae non adhibeantur artes, tamen facile declaratur, utrum is, qui dicat, tantum modo in hoc declamatorio sit opere iactatus an ad dicendum omnibus ingenuis artibus instructus accesserit."

In the third book, XX and subsequent chapters, Crassus takes up the theme of the importance of good education. In paragraphs 74-81, he made his own some of Antonius' observations, who had emphasized the need for practical skills, our *soft skills*, to be able to overcome forensic lawsuits and, in general, to impose and make successful one's own point of view. Antonius had also questioned the real possibility that one person could have the cultural heritage to which Crassus had attached so much importance.

Crassus provides proof of his ability in the debate by retracing and partially accepting Antonius' right criticisms. Indeed, his first defensive argument is to affirm that he is prefiguring a model of perfection to be achieved, but of which he does not feel the incarnation at all. On the other hand, he reiterates that he began his glorious career when he was only 21 years old against a skilled opponent such as Gaius Papirius Carbo and he claims to be a man «cui disciplina fuerit forum, magister usus et leges et instituta populi Romani mosque maiorum...nam neque sine forensibus nervis satis vehemens et gravis nec sine varietate doctrinae satis politus et sapiens esse orator potest» («who had the Forum for the training, the practice, the laws, the institutions of the Roman people and the ancestral costumes as teachers... indeed the orator cannot be convincing and authoritative enough without strong

nerves for the Forum, cannot be elegant and wise enough without the variety of culture»).

The orator / politician takes the form of a man of law, devoted to his country and his *mores*, and man of letters: a simple and clear description of a non-bookish education, but cultural in the broadest sense of the term.

[XX] [74] Quae cum ita sint, paululum equidem de me deprecabor et petam a vobis, ut ea, quae dicam, non de memet ipso, sed de oratore dicere putetis. Ego enim sum is, qui cum summo studio patris in pueritia doctus essem et in forum ingeni tantum, quantum ipse sentio, non tantum, quantum [ipse] forsitan vobis videar, detulissem, non possim dicere me haec, quae nunc complector, perinde, ut dicam discenda esse, didicisse; quippe qui omnium maturrime ad publicas causas accesserim annosque natus unum et viginti nobilissimum hominem et eloquentissimum in iudicium vocarim; cui disciplina fuerit forum, magister usus et leges et instituta Populi Romani mosque maiorum. [75] Paulum sitiens istarum artium, de quibus loquor, gustavi, quaestor

in Asia cum essem, aequalem fere meum ex
Academia rhetorem nactus, Metrodorum illum, de
cuius memoria commemoravit Antonius; et inde
decedens Athenis, ubi ego diutius essem moratus,
nisi Atheniensibus, quod mysteria non referrent, ad
quae biduo serius veneram, suscensuissem; qua re
hoc, quod complector tantam scientiam vimque
doctrinae, non modo non pro me, sed contra me est
potius - non enim quid ego, sed quid orator possit
disputo - atque hos omnis, qui artis rhetoricas
exponunt, perridiculos; scribunt enim de litium
genere et de principiis et de narrationibus; [76] illa
vis autem eloquentiae tanta est, ut omnium rerum,
virtutum, officiorum omnisque naturae, quae mores
hominum, quae animos, quae vitam continet,
originem, vim mutationesque teneat, eadem mores,
leges, iura describat, rem publicam regat, omniaque,
ad quamcumque rem pertineant, ornate copioseque
dicat. [77] In quo genere nos quidem versamur
tantum quantum possumus, quantum ingenio,
quantum mediocri doctrina, quantum usu valemus;
neque tamen istis, qui in una philosophia quasi
tabernaculum vitae suae conlocarunt, multum sane
in disputatione concedimus.

[XXI] [78] Quid enim meus familiaris C. Velleius adferre potest, quam ob rem voluptas sit summum bonum, quod ego non copiosius possim vel tutari, si velim, vel refellere ex illis locis, quos euit Antonius, hac dicendi exercitatione, in qua Velleius est rudis, unus quisque nostrum versatus? Quid est, quod aut Sex. Pompeius aut duo Balbi aut meus amicus, qui cum Panaetio vixit, M. Vigellius de virtute hominum Stoici possint dicere, qua in disputatione ego his debeam aut vestrum quisquam concedere? [79] Non est enim philosophia similis artium reliquarum: nam quid faciet in geometria qui non didicerit? Quid in musicis? Aut taceat oportebit aut ne sanus quidem iudicetur. Haec vero, quae sunt in philosophia, ingeniis eruuntur ad id, quod in quoque veri simile est, eliciendum acutis atque acribus eaque exercitata oratione poliuntur. Hic noster vulgaris orator, si minus erit doctus, at tamen in dicendo exercitatus, hac ipsa exercitatione communi istos quidem [nostros] verberabit neque se ab eis contemni ac despici sinet; [80] sin aliquis exstiterit aliquando, qui Aristotelio more de omnibus rebus in utramque partem possit dicere et in omni causa duas contrarias orationes, praeceptis illius cognitis, explicare aut hoc

Arcesilae modo et Carneadi contra omne, quod propositum sit, disserat, quique ad eam rationem adiungat hunc [rhetoricum] usum [moremque] exercitationemque dicendi, is sit verus, is perfectus, is solus orator. Nam neque sine forensibus nervis satis vehemens et gravis nec sine varietate doctrinae satis politus et sapiens esse orator potest. [81] Qua re Coracem istum veterem patiamur nos quidem pullos suos excludere in nido, qui evolent clamatores odiosi ac molesti, Pamphilumque nescio quem sinamus in infulis tantam rem tamquam puerilis delicias aliquas depingere; nosque ipsi hac tam exigua disputatione hesterni et hodierni diei totum oratoris munus explicemus, dum modo illa res tanta sit, ut omnibus philosophorum libris, quos nemo [oratorum] istorum umquam attigit, comprehensa esse videatur."

In the following paragraphs of the third book, in particular §88 and 89, Crassus clarifies that culture must be wider than deep, so that at the right moment the fact of being equipped with 'tools' to study any discipline, allows the orator to deepen if necessary. The assiduous study indeed allows you to learn

faster and more easily and this is the measure of the validity of your method.

This pedagogical reflection is particularly significant, as Augusto Rostagni already warned, since discussions continue on the validity of high school disciplines, and in particular on Greek and Latin, for professional training. After all, we often hear that those who have to make calculations to build a palace need not poetry or literature. Crassus, who is Cicero's voice, is responding to this objection with the simple observation of the fact that a beautiful and well done building is destined to be long inhabited and to last and that calculations are not enough to give beauty to a building. This is the value of culture. Thoughts, exactly as objects, exist regardless of our ability to narrate and describe, but it is our ability to express «recte et ornate» thoughts that give them value and it allows a wider sharing.

[88] sed si tota vita nihil velis aliud agere, ipsa tractatio et quaestio cotidie ex se gignit aliquid, quod cum desidiosa delectatione vestiges. Ita fit, ut agitatio rerum sit infinita, cognitio facilis, si usus doctrinam

confirmet, mediocris opera tribuatur, memoria studiumque permaneat. **Libet autem semper discere**; ut si velim ego talis optime ludere aut pilae studio tenear, etiam fortasse, si adsequi non possim; at alii, quia praeclare faciunt, vehementius, quam causa postulat, delectantur, ut Titius pila, Brulla talis. [89] Qua re nihil est quod quisquam magnitudinem artium ex eo, quod senes discunt, pertimescat, namque aut senes ad eas accesserunt aut usque ad senectutem in studiis detinentur aut sunt tardissimi; res quidem se mea sententia sic habet, ut **nisi quod quisque cito potuerit, numquam omnino possit perdiscere**."

And now, with chapters 109-117 of Third book we go into a very technical but extremely interesting section of *De Oratore*, in which Crassus deals with political philosophy.

The starting point appears very simple: the *loci communes*, that is, the set of arguments that serve to reinforce a reasoning, clarifying it with obvious examples and within everyone's reach.

The speech becomes complicated when Crassus says that the "political" philosophers, so called by the Greeks because of their knowledge of the dynamics of the States, have claimed for themselves the exclusive prerogative of the teaching of these *loci communes* as reasoning techniques. Crassus demonstrates how it is the orator, rather than the philosopher, the person who masters this matter, and he does it with his style with a small 'treatise' on the techniques of argumentation.

Crassus says that 2 can be the <u>aims</u> of an investigation:

a: verification of the facts;

b: search for a norm to act.

The <u>investigation</u> itself is divided into:

a: conjectures;

b: definitions;

c: consequences.

<u>Conjectures</u> used to determine:

a: what a thing is;

b: the origin of a thing;

c: the causes;

d: the changes.

<u>Definitions</u> are divided into:

a: common opinions;

b: assessment of what is proper to an object of study;

c: division into parts of the object of investigation;

d: description of the particularities of a study object.

<u>Consequences</u> are divided into:

a: simple discussions;

b: comparisons.

<u>Simple discussions</u> aim to establish:

a: what to look for and what to avoid;

b: what is fair and what is unfair;

c: what is honourable and what is foul.

<u>Comparisons</u> instead aim to establish:

a: if 2 things are either the same or different in some aspect;

b: what is preferable between 2 things.

[104] Summa autem laus eloquentiae est amplificare rem ornando, quod valet non solum ad augendum aliquid et tollendum altius dicendo, sed etiam ad extenuandum atque abiciendum.

[XXVII] Id desideratur omnibus eis in locis, quos ad fidem orationis faciendam adhiberi dixit Antonius, vel cum explanamus aliquid vel cum conciliamus animos vel cum concitamus; [105] sed in hoc, quod postremum dixi, amplificatio potest plurimum, eaque una laus oratoris est [et] propria maxime. Etiam maior est illa exercitatio quam extremo sermone instruxit Antonius, primo reiciebat, laudandi et vituperandi; nihil est enim ad exaggerandam et amplificandam orationem accommodatius, quam utrumque horum cumulatissime facere posse. [106] Consequentur etiam illi loci, qui quamquam proprii causarum et inhaerentes in earum nervis esse debent, tamen quia de universa re tractari solent, communes a veteribus nominati sunt; quorum partim habent vitiorum et peccatorum acrem quandam cum amplificatione incusationem aut querelam, contra quam dici nihil solet nec potest, ut in depeculatorem, in proditorem, in parricidam; quibus uti confirmatis criminibus oportet, aliter enim ieiuni sunt atque inanes; [107] alii autem habent deprecationem aut miserationem; alii vero ancipitis disputationes, in quibus de universo genere in utramque partem disseri copiose licet. Quae exercitatio nunc propria duarum philosophiarum, de quibus ante dixi, putatur, apud antiquos erat eorum, a quibus omnis de rebus forensibus dicendi ratio et copia petebatur; de virtute enim, de officio, de aequo et bono, de dignitate, utilitate, honore, ignominia, praemio, poena similibusque de rebus in utramque partem dicendi etiam nos et vim et artem habere debemus. [108] Sed quoniam de nostra possessione depulsi in parvo et eo litigioso praediolo relicti sumus et aliorum patroni nostra tenere tuerique non potuimus, ab eis, quod indignissimum est, qui in nostrum patrimonium inruperunt, quod opus est nobis mutuemur.

[XXVIII] [109] Dicunt igitur nunc quidem illi, qui ex particula parva urbis ac loci nomen habent et Peripatetici philosophi aut Academici nominantur, olim autem propter eximiam rerum maximarum scientiam a Graecis politici philosophi appellati universarum rerum publicarum nomine vocabantur, omnem civilem orationem in horum alterutro genere versari: aut de finita controversia certis temporibus ac reis; hoc modo: placeatne a Karthaginiensibus captivos nostros redditis suis recuperari? Aut infinite de universo genere quaerentis: quid omnino de captivo statuendum ac sentiendum sit? Atque horum superius illud genus causam aut controversiam appellant eamque tribus, lite aut deliberatione aut laudatione, definiunt; haec autem altera quaestio infinita et quasi proposita consultatio nominatur. [110] Atque [hactenus loquantur] etiam hac in instituendo divisione utuntur, sed ita, non ut iure aut iudicio, vi denique recuperare amissam possessionem, sed ut [iure civili] surculo defringendo usurpare videantur. Nam illud alterum genus, quod est temporibus, locis, reis definitum, obtinent, atque id ipsum lacinia - nunc enim apud Philonem, quem in Academia [maxime] vigere audio, etiam harum iam causarum cognitio exercitatioque celebratur - alterum vero tantum modo in prima arte tradenda nominant et oratoris esse dicunt; sed neque vim neque naturam eius nec partis nec genera proponunt, ut praeteriri omnino fuerit satius quam attactum deseri; nunc enim inopia reticere intelleguntur, tum iudicio viderentur.

[XXIX] [111] Omnis igitur res eandem habet naturam ambigendi, de qua quaeri et disceptari potest, sive in infinitis consultationibus disceptatur sive in eis causis, quae in civitate et forensi disceptatione versantur; neque est ulla, quae non aut ad cognoscendi aut ad agendi vim rationemque referatur; [112] nam aut ipsa cognitio rei scientiaque perquiritur, ut virtus suamne propter dignitatem an propter fructum aliquem expetatur; aut agendi consilium exquiritur, ut sitne sapienti capessenda res publica. [113] Cognitionis autem tres modi, coniectura, definitio et, ut ita dicam, consecutio: nam quid in re sit, coniectura quaeritur, ut illud, sitne in humano genere sapientia, quam autem vim quaeque res habeat, definitio explicat, ut si quaeratur, quid sit sapientia; consecutio autem tractatur, cum quid quamque rem sequatur, anquiritur, ut illud, sitne aliquando mentiri boni viri. [114] Redeunt rursus ad coniecturam eamque in quattuor genera dispertiunt; nam aut quid sit quaeritur, hoc modo: naturane sit ius inter homines an in opinionibus; aut, quae sit origo cuiusque rei, ut quod sit initium legum aut rerum publicarum; aut causa et ratio, ut si quaeratur, cur doctissimi homines de maximis rebus dissentiant; aut de immutatione, ut, si disputetur, num interire virtus in homine aut num in vitium possit convertere. [115] Definitionis autem sunt disceptationes aut, cum quaeritur, quid in communi mente quasi impressum sit, ut si disseratur, idne sit ius, quod maximae parti sit utile; aut, cum quid cuiusque sit proprium exquiritur, ut ornate dicere propriumne sit oratoris an id etiam aliquis praeterea facere possit, aut? cum res distribuitur in partis, ut si quaeratur, quot sint genera rerum expetendarum, ut sintne tria, corporis, animi externarumque rerum, aut, cum, quae forma et quasi naturalis nota cuiusque sit, describitur, ut si quaeratur avari species, seditiosi, gloriosi. [116] Consecutionis autem duo prima quaestionum genera ponuntur; nam aut simplex est disceptatio, ut si disseratur, expetendane sit gloria, aut ex comparatione, laus an divitiae magis expetendae sint; simplicium autem sunt tres modi: de expetendis fugiendisve rebus, ut expetendine honores sint, num fugienda paupertas; de aequo aut iniquo, ut aequumne sit ulcisci iniurias etiam propinquorum; de honesto aut turpi, ut hoc, sitne honestum gloriae causa mortem obire. [117] Comparationis autem duo sunt modi: unus, cum idemne sit an aliquid intersit quaeritur; ut metuere et vereri, ut rex et tyrannus, ut adsentator et amicus; alter, cum quid praestet aliud alii quaeritur, ut illud, optimine cuiusque sapientes an populari laude ducantur. Atque eae quidem disceptationes, quae ad cognitionem referuntur, sic fere a doctissimis hominibus describuntur.

[XXX] [118] Quae vero referuntur ad agendum, aut in offici disceptatione versantur, quo in genere quid rectum faciendumque sit quaeritur, cui loco omnis virtutum et vitiorum est silva subiecta, aut in animorum aliqua permotione aut gignenda aut sedanda tollendave tractantur. Huic generi subiectae sunt cohortationes, obiurgationes, consolationes, miserationes omnisque ad omnem animi motum et impulsio et, si ita res feret, mitigatio. [119] Explicatis igitur his generibus ac modis disceptationum omnium nihil sane ad rem pertinet, si qua in re discrepavit ab Antoni divisione nostra partitio: eadem sunt membra in utriusque disputatione, sed paulo secus a me atque ab illo partita ac tributa. Nunc ad reliqua progrediar meque ad meum munus pensumque revocabo. Nam ex illis locis, quos euit Antonius, omnia sunt ad quaeque genera quaestionum argumenta sumenda; sed aliis generibus alii loci magis erunt apti; de quo non tam quia longum est quam quia perspicuum est, dici nihil est necesse. [120] Ornatissimae sunt igitur orationes eae, quae latissime vagantur et a privata [et a singulari] controversia se ad universi generis vim explicandam conferunt et convertunt, ut ei, qui audiant, natura et genere et universa re cognita de singulis reis et criminibus et litibus statuere possint. [121] Hanc ad consuetudinem exercitationis vos, adulescentes, est cohortatus Antonius atque a minutis angustisque concertationibus ad omnem vim varietatemque vos disserendi traducendos putavit; qua re non est paucorum libellorum hoc munus, ut ei, qui scripserunt de dicendi ratione, arbitrantur, neque Tusculani atque huius ambulationis antemeridianae aut nostrae posmeridianae sessionis; non enim solum acuenda nobis neque procudenda lingua est, sed onerandum complendumque pectus maximarum rerum et plurimarum suavitate, copia, varietate.

[XXXI] [122] Nostra est enim - si modo nos oratores, si in civium disceptationibus, si in periculis, si in deliberationibus publicis adhibendi auctores et principes sumus - nostra est, inquam, omnis ista prudentiae doctrinaeque possessio, in quam homines quasi caducam atque vacuam abundantes otio, nobis occupatis, involaverunt atque etiam aut inridentes oratorem, ut ille in Gorgia Socrates, cavillantur aut aliquid de oratoris arte paucis praecipiunt libellis eosque rhetoricos inscribunt, quasi non illa sint propria rhetorum, quae ab eisdem de iustitia, de officio, de civitatibus instituendis et regendis, de omni vivendi denique etiam de naturae ratione dicuntur. [123] Quae quoniam iam aliunde non possumus, sumenda sunt nobis ab eis ipsis, a quibus expilati sumus; dum modo illa ad hanc civilem scientiam, quo pertinent et quam intuentur, transferamus, neque, ut ante dixi, omnem teramus in his discendis rebus aetatem; sed cum fontis viderimus, quos nisi qui celeriter cognorit, numquam cognoscet omnino, tum, quotienscumque opus erit, ex eis tantum, quantum res petet, hauriemus; [124] nam neque tam est acris acies in naturis hominum et ingeniis, ut res tantas quisquam nisi monstratas possit videre, neque tanta tamen in rebus obscuritas, ut eas non penitus acri vir ingenio cernat, si modo aspexerit. In hoc igitur tanto tam immensoque campo cum liceat oratori vagari libere atque ubicumque constiterit, consistere in suo, facile suppeditat omnis apparatus ornatusque dicendi; [125] rerum enim copia verborum copiam gignit; et, si est honestas in rebus ipsis, de quibus dicitur, exsistit ex re naturalis quidam splendor in verbis. Sit modo is, qui dicet aut scribet, institutus liberaliter educatione doctrinaque puerili et flagret studio et a natura adiuvetur et in universorum generum infinitis disceptationibus exercitatus ornatissimos scriptores oratoresque ad cognoscendum imitandumque delegerit, ne ille haud sane, quem ad modum verba struat et inluminet, a magistris istis requiret; ita facile in rerum abundantia ad orationis ornamenta sine duce natura ipsa, si modo est exercitata, delabitur."

After examining technical aspects, Crassus - in chapters 126-131- praises the ancient orators for their extreme versatility. Hippias of Elis, for example, owes his fame both to the vast knowledge of the «artes liberales» that is, geometry, music, literature and poetry, sciences (natural, moral and political sciences), and to his ability to manufacture himself a cloak and sandals. Here is a sincere praise of the great Greek orators ... of the past! Of the past only because the passage ends with an open and poisonous criticism of the Greeks of his time who, despite having the good fortune to be born among literary works and already endowed with a burning love for all the arts, have the serious defect to be lazy, so not only have they not added anything to what has been handed down but they are not even able to preserve their heritage.

[XXXII] [126] Hic Catulus "di immortales," inquit "quantam rerum varietatem, quantam vim, quantam copiam, Crasse, complexus es quantisque ex angustiis oratorem educere ausus es et in maiorum suorum regno conlocare! Namque illos veteres doctores auctoresque dicendi nullum genus disputationis a se alienum putasse accepimus semperque esse in omni orationis ratione versatos; [127] ex quibus Elius Hippias, cum Olympiam venisset maxima illa quinquennali celebritate ludorum, gloriatus est cuncta paene audiente Graecia nihil esse ulla in arte rerum omnium quod ipse nesciret; nec solum has artis, quibus liberales doctrinae atque ingenuae continerentur, geometriam, musicam, litterarum cognitionem et poetarum atque illa, quae de naturis rerum, quae de hominum moribus, quae de rebus publicis dicerentur, se tenere sed anulum, quem haberet, pallium, quo amictus, soccos, quibus indutus esset, [se] sua manu confecisse. [128] Scilicet nimis hic quidem est progressus, sed ex eo ipso est coniectura facilis, quantum sibi illi oratores de praeclarissimis artibus appetierint, qui ne sordidiores quidem repudiarint. Quid de Prodico Cio, de Thrasymacho Calchedonio, de Protagora Abderita loquar? Quorum unus quisque plurimum ut temporibus illis etiam de natura rerum et disseruit et scripsit. [129] Ipse ille Leontinus Gorgias, quo patrono, ut Plato voluit, philosopho succubuit orator, qui aut non est victus umquam a Socrate neque sermo ille Platonis verus est; aut, si est victus, eloquentior videlicet fuit et disertior Socrates et, ut tu appellas, copiosior et melior orator - sed hic in illo ipso Platonis libro de omni re, quaecumque in disceptationem quaestionemque vocetur, se copiosissime dicturum esse profitetur; isque princeps ex omnibus ausus est in conventu poscere qua de re quisque vellet audire; cui tantus honos habitus est a Graecia, soli ut ex omnibus Delphis non inaurata statua sed aurea statueretur. [130] Sed hi, quos nominavi, multique praeterea summique dicendi doctores uno tempore fuerunt; ex quibus intellegi potest ita se rem habere, ut tu, Crasse, dicis, oratorisque nomen apud antiquos in Graecia maiore quadam vel copia vel gloria floruisse. [131] Quo quidem magis dubito tibine plus laudis an Graecis vituperationis statuam esse tribuendum: cum tu in alia lingua ac moribus natus occupatissima in civitate vel privatorum negotiis paene omnibus vel orbis terrae procuratione ac summi imperi gubernatione destrictus tantam vim rerum cognitionemque comprehenderis eamque omnem cum eius, qui consilio et oratione in civitate valeat, scientia atque exercitatione sociaris; illi nati in litteris ardentesque his studiis, otio vero diffluentes, non modo nihil acquisierint, sed ne relictum quidem et traditum et suum conservarint."

I conclude this short anthology with the praise of some Roman orators and politicians of the past who are compared to characters from his present. The difference lies in the fact that in his time public figures always had a sort of «incomplete armour»: either were they educated men, or had only one good quality. Consequently, they are not considered true statesmen because only those who truly grasp the link between the liberal arts are able to grasp the link between the virtues and make them what for Crassus, as for Ciccro, was the best use: to put his own person,

with experience and culture, at the service of the
State.

De Oratore III, 134-143

[134] Haec fuit P. Crassi illius veteris, haec Ti. Coruncani, haec proavi generi mei Scipionis prudentissimi hominis sapientia, qui omnes pontifices maximi fuerunt, ut ad eos de omnibus divinis atque humanis rebus referretur; eidemque in senatu et apud populum et in causis amicorum et domi et militiae consilium suum fidemque praestabant. [135] Quid enim M. Catoni praeter hanc politissimam doctrinam transmarinam atque adventiciam defuit? Num, quia ius civile didicerat, causas non dicebat? Aut quia poterat dicere, iuris scientiam neglegebat? Vtroque in genere et elaboravit et praestitit. Num propter hanc ex privatorum negotiis conlectam gratiam tardior in re publica capessenda fuit? Nemo apud populum fortior, nemo melior senator; et idem facile optimus imperator; denique nihil in hac civitate temporibus illis sciri discive potuit, quod ille non cum investigarit et

scierit tum etiam conscripserit. [136] Nunc contra plerique ad honores adipiscendos et ad rem publicam gerendam nudi veniunt atque inermes, nulla cognitione rerum, nulla scientia ornati. Sin aliquis excellit unus e multis, effert se, si unum aliquid adfert, aut bellicam virtutem aut usum aliquem militarem; quae sane nunc quidem obsoleverunt; aut iuris scientiam, ne eius quidem universi; nam pontificium, quod est coniunctum, nemo discit; aut eloquentiam, quam in clamore et in verborum cursu positam putant; omnium vero bonarum artium, denique virtutum ipsarum societatem cognationemque non norunt.

[136] Nunc contra plerique ad honores adipiscendos et ad rem publicam gerendam nudi veniunt atque inermes, nulla cognitione rerum, nulla scientia ornati. Sin aliquis excellit unus e multis, effert se, si unum aliquid adfert, aut bellicam virtutem aut usum aliquem militarem; quae sane nunc quidem obsoleverunt; aut iuris scientiam, ne eius quidem universi; nam pontificium, quod est coniunctum, nemo discit; aut eloquentiam, quam in clamore et in verborum cursu positam putant; omnium vero

bonarum artium, denique virtutum ipsarum societatem cognationemque non norunt.

[XXXIV] [137] Sed ut ad Graecos referam orationem, quibus carere hoc quidem in sermonis genere non possumus - nam ut virtutis a nostris, sic doctrinae sunt ab illis exempla petenda - septem fuisse dicuntur uno tempore, qui sapientes et haberentur et vocarentur: hi omnes praeter Milesium Thalen civitatibus suis praefuerunt. Quis doctior eisdem temporibus illis aut cuius eloquentia litteris instructior fuisse traditur quam Pisistrati? Qui primus Homeri libros confusos antea sic disposuisse dicitur, ut nunc habemus. Non fuit ille quidem civibus suis utilis, sed ita eloquentia floruit, ut litteris doctrinaque praestaret. [138] Quid Pericles? De cuius vi dicendi sic accepimus, ut, cum contra voluntatem Atheniensium loqueretur pro salute patriae severius, tamen id ipsum, quod ille contra popularis homines diceret, populare omnibus et iucundum videretur; cuius in labris veteres comici, etiam cum illi male dicerent (quod tum Athenis fieri licebat), leporem habitasse dixerunt tantamque in eodem vim fuisse, ut in eorum mentibus, qui audissent, quasi aculeos quosdam relinqueret. At hunc non declamator aliqui ad clepsydram latrare docuerat, sed, ut accepimus, Clazomenius ille Anaxagoras vir summus in maximarum rerum scientia: itaque hic doctrina, consilio, eloquentia excellens quadraginta annis praefuit Athenis et urbanis eodem tempore et bellicis rebus. [139] Quid Critias? Quid Alcibiades? Civitatibus quidem suis non boni, sed certe docti atque eloquentes, nonne Socraticis erant disputationibus eruditi? Quis Dionem Syracosium doctrinis omnibus expolivit? Non Plato? Atque eum idem ille non linguae solum, verum etiam animi ac virtutis magister ad liberandam patriam impulit, instruxit, armavit. Aliisne igitur artibus hunc Dionem instituit Plato, aliis Isocrates clarissimum virum Timotheum Cononis praestantissimi imperatoris filium, summum ipsum imperatorem hominemque doctissimum? Aut aliis Pythagorius ille Lysis Thebanum Epaminondam, haud scio an summum virum unum omnis Graeciae? Aut Xenophon Agesilaum? Aut Philolaus Archytam Tarentinum? Aut ipse Pythagoras totam illam veterem Italiae Graeciam, quae quondam magna vocitata est?

[XXXV] [140] Equidem non arbitror; sic enim video, unam quandam omnium rerum, quae essent homine erudito dignae atque eo, qui in re publica vellet excellere, fuisse doctrinam; quam qui accepissent, si eidem ingenio ad pronuntiandum valuissent et se ad dicendum quoque non repugnante natura dedissent, eloquentia praestitisse. [141] Itaque ipse Aristoteles cum florere Isocratem nobilitate discipulorum videret, quod [ipse] suas disputationes a causis forensibus et civilibus ad inanem sermonis elegantiam transtulisset, mutavit repente totam formam prope disciplinae suae versumque quendam Philoctetae paulo secus dixit: ille enim turpe sibi ait esse tacere, cum barbaros, hic autem, cum Isocratem pateretur dicere; itaque ornavit et inlustravit doctrinam illam omnem rerumque cognitionem cum orationis exercitatione coniunxit. Neque vero hoc fugit sapientissimum regem Philippum, qui hunc Alexandro filio doctorem accierit, a quo eodem ille et agendi acciperet praecepta et eloquendi. [142] Nunc sive qui volet, eum philosophum, qui copiam nobis rerum orationisque tradat, per me appellet oratorem licet; sive hunc oratorem, quem ego dico sapientiam iunctam habere eloquentiae, philosophum appellare malet, non impediam; dum modo hoc constet, neque infantiam eius, qui rem norit, sed eam explicare dicendo non queat, neque inscientiam illius, cui res non suppetat, verba non desint, esse laudandam; quorum si alterum sit optandum, **malim equidem indisertam prudentiam quam stultitiam loquacem**; [143] sin quaerimus quid unum excellat ex omnibus, docto oratori palma danda est; quem si patiuntur eundem esse philosophum, sublata controversia est; sin eos diiungent, hoc erunt inferiores, quod in oratore perfecto inest illorum omnis scientia, in philosophorum autem cognitione non continuo inest eloquentia; quae quamvis contemnatur ab eis, necesse est tamen aliquem cumulum illorum artibus adferre videatur."